The Big brown pot

Written by Margaret Mahy

Illustrated by Deborah Rigby

One sunny day, Mr Winkle woke up early.
He put on his chef's hat and apron, and began
to make a stew in his big brown pot.

Mr Winkle added a pinch of this
and a pinch of that to the pot.
He chopped and stirred. The stew bubbled
and boiled. Soon it smelled delicious.

"This stew would be better if I shared it,"
Mr Winkle said to himself. "I will go to visit
my friend, Tom, and take the stew with me."

Mr Winkle went out to his tiny red car.
He put the big brown pot on the roof
of the car while he opened the door.
Then he got in the car and drove away.

As Mr Winkle drove down the lane, two dogs
caught a whiff of the stew. They sniffed
and sniffed. It smelled wonderful. The two dogs
chased the tiny red car.

The dog-catcher saw the two dogs chasing
Mr Winkle's car.

"I'd better catch those dogs!" she announced,
and she immediately drove off in her
dog-catcher's van.

Just then, Mrs Bright peeked out of the window and saw the dog-catcher following the two dogs. "Those are my dogs!" she cried. "I must tell the dog-catcher."

Mrs Bright grabbed her helmet and climbed on her scooter. Off she sped, following the dog-catcher, who was following the dogs, who were following the wonderful-smelling stew in the big brown pot on the roof of the tiny red car.

Just then the police were driving by
in their police car. "What's going on?"
they said. "We'd better find out!"

So the police followed Mrs Bright,
who was following the dog-catcher, who was
following the dogs, who were following
the wonderful-smelling stew in the big
brown pot on the roof of the tiny red car.

As Mr Winkle neared his friend's house, he suddenly remembered, "Oh no! Today is Friday. Tom is at work! I'd better go home. How sad it is that there is no one to share my wonderful stew."

Mr Winkle drove all the way home and stopped outside his own house.

the two dogs, the dog-catcher, Mrs Bright
and the police stopped near the tiny red car.
Mr Winkle was searching for the stew.
He looked on the front seat and the back
seat, but it wasn't there.

"My delicious stew has disappeared,"
cried Mr Winkle.

Everyone pointed and shouted, "Look on
the roof of your car, Mr Winkle!"

"There it is," said Mr Winkle. "Is anybody hungry?"

"I am!" shouted the dog-catcher.

"I am!" cried Mrs Bright.

"We are!" agreed the police officers.

"Woof, woof!" barked the two dogs.

"Then come inside and share my delicious stew,"
said Mr Winkle. "There is plenty for everyone."

A Parcel for
Wilma W. Willis

Written by Janine Scott

Illustrated by Ian Forss

If your mother asks you to post
a parcel to her friend, Wilma W. Willis
the walrus, please check what is inside
it before you take it to the post office.
Otherwise, the postal worker could get
a fright when the parcel flips and flops
along the counter into the postie's bag.

Unaware of what is inside his bag,
the postie could be chased by cats.
The poor postie could be allergic to cats.
He might let out the wheeziest sneeze.
The cats and the parcel could go flying
up into the nearest tree.

Before long, a mama bird might come
back and think there is a strange chick
sitting in her nest. She might pick up
the funny-shaped chick in her beak
and throw it out of the nest.

A car might be driving by. The parcel could land on the car's roof. The polar bear driving the car might not realise why people were waving their arms and yelling at her. She might just smile and wave back.

When the driver parks outside a fish market,
the parcel could slide and slip into an old bear's
basket. He might be buying his dinner.

The old bear might not notice the parcel
flipping and flopping out of his basket into
a truck at the fish market. The parcel could
flip and flop with the fish on their way
to a fish restaurant. The parcel might sense danger.
It then might flip and flop out of the truck.

the truck could be passing a river
at that very moment. The parcel could end
up flipping and flopping down the river,
all the way to 2 Water Lane. It could land
on Wilma W. Willis's icy cold doorstep.

Ideas for Parents

- Reading with children is an important way of encouraging a love of books. It familiarises your child with the patterns of the written language and helps increase his or her vocabulary, assisting him or her on the road to literacy.

- Urge your child to join in with reading. Encourage him or her to finish sentences, try new words and read sections on his or her own. Always read the book a number of times. Repetition familiarises children with language patterns and makes it more likely that they will join in.

- Children learn best when an experience is enjoyable, so always make reading together a positive and fun experience.

Helping Children to Understand the Text and Build Reading Skills

The Big Brown Pot

- As you read together, ask questions that encourage your child to search the pictures or scan the words for clues to the answers, such as:
  What do you think Mr Winkle is going to make?
  What sort of a person do you think Mr Winkle is? Why?
  Why did the dogs chase the car?
  Why did Mrs Bright chase the dogs?

- Discuss how the story ends. Ask: *Is this a good ending? Why?*

A Parcel for Wilma W. Willis

- Start by asking why it would be a good idea to check a parcel being sent to a walrus. Then enjoy the whimsical text and illustrations together.

- Point out the use of alliteration, and the way the author repeats sounds to help create impact throughout the story. Repeat some of the alliterative phrases and see if your child can hear and identify the starting letters or blends, such as: *friend/fright, flip/flop, slip/slide.*

- Discuss the ending of the story. Ask how the story might continue if the next parcel was posted.

So please, please, please, remember, if your mother asks you to post a fly-shaped parcel to her froggy friend, Freddy F. Franklin, please, please, don't even think about it. Get the parcel to fly airmail instead!

When she opens the parcel, a fish could flop out.
Wilma W. Willis might say, "Oh, a flipping fish!
This isn't my parcel. I was waiting for a clam.
I will have to send the parcel back!"

Wilma W. Willis might take the flipping, flopping parcel into her house, but she might be puzzled by its shape.